Where Do Recyclable Materials Go?

by Sabbithry Persad

ECOADVENTURES

An imprint of **Firewater Media Group**

Orlando • Toronto

Several people have helped in vetting the content of this book. In particular, our sincere thanks go to Dr. Robin Nagle (Anthropologist, New York University), Josephine Valencia (Solid Waste Disposal Manager, City of Durham, North Carolina), Dr. Susanne Rotter (Professor for Solid Waste Management, Berlin University of Technology, Germany) and Mike Webster (Senior Consultant, Waste Watch UK) for their enthusiastic and informed reviews.

Special thanks to my friends and everyone who participated in the making of this book, especially Emma, Franfou Studio for initial storyboard and illustrations and W. Kimber for reillustrating them in his style.

Library and Archives Canada Cataloguing in Publication

Persad, Sabbithry, 1971-
Garbology kids : where do recyclable materials go? / Persad Sabbithry.

(Garbology kids series)
ISBN 978-0-9812439-0-0

I. Title. II. Series : Garbology kids series.

PS8631.E785T75 2010   jC813'.6   C2010-901105-8

Publisher's Cataloging-In-Publication Data (U.S.)
(Prepared by The Donohue Group, Inc.)

Persad, Sabbithry.
Where do recyclable materials go? / by Sabbithry Persad.

p. : col. ill. ; cm. -- (Garbology kids)

Summary: Tiana shares with her class what she learned about recycling
while trying to catch her dog Bubbles, who ran after the recycling truck.
"Read, think, recycle."--Cover.
"Ecoadventures."--T.p.
ISBN: 978-0-9812439-0-0

1. Recycling (Waste, etc.)--Juvenile literature. 2. Recycling (Waste) I. Title. II. Series: Garbology kids

TD792 .P47 2011
628.4/458   2010924659

Library of Congress Control Number: 2010924659

6 5 4 3 2   Printed in Canada   10 11 12 13 14 15

This text and cover has been printed locally on environmentally-friendly paper — FSC® certified, acid-free, elemental chlorine free (ECF) and recyclable.

Where Do Recyclable Materials Go?

For my parents Jean and Ramsaran ... and my siblings, nieces and nephews.
Thanks for the continued support.

At school we had been learning about waste and landfills. I was curious about recycling and wanted to learn more about it.

Then one morning my dog Bubbles ran after the recycle truck and I learned a lot more when my family and I had to find her.

At breakfast that day, I asked Mom, "Doesn't Bubbles need to go to the groomer today?"

"Yes! Let's bring her inside before she chases the recycle truck again. We don't want to miss her hair trimming with Mr. Mendez this afternoon."

But when I went out to the yard to get her, she wasn't there!

Bubbles! BUBBLES! Come on, girl!

More and more cities are introducing offering recycling services but not all have it yet. However in some places it's the law.

"Bubbles is gone!" I cried.

"We have to find her!" yelled my younger brother, Peter.

"Don't worry," Mom said. "We'll find her. Let's start checking the recycle truck's pick up stops right away. Can you both help me carry this bag of recyclable materials to the car?"

"Sure, Mom!" I looked at the bag. "What are recyclable materials?"

"Reusable resources—everything we might throw out that can be used to make new products again."

"Is that what we put in the new 'recycle bin' at the curb?" asked Peter.

"That's right. Recycle collectors pick them up then drive them away in their recycle truck."

"But where do they take all that stuff?" I asked.
"To the MURF!" Mom said.
"To the what? What's a MURF?" Peter and I giggled at the funny-sounding word.
"The MURF is the M.R.F. It's short for Materials Recovery Facility, but sometimes we call it the Recycling Facility."

I looked inside the bag. "How do we know what to put in the bin?"

"Well, tell me what you see in there."

"Um…pop bottles, juice bottles and jars." I pulled out a soup can. "And cans."

Peter shoved his head into the bag.

"Hey," he mumbled, "there's a whole pile of newspapers in here!"

"Yup, you're both right," Mom said. "Plastic, glass, metal and paper are all recyclable materials. What looks like waste to us will all be made into new things."

Some things like appliances, electronics, furniture or hazardous materials cannot go in the recycle bin or waste bin. Many cities have a collection program to take them to a special depot.

"They all go in our recycle bin, then to the MURF," Mom continued. "We forgot to put out our bin for pick-up last night. So, let's find Bubbles first, then take them to the MURF ourselves."

Peter and I put the recycle bin in the trunk and Mom drove to the animal shelter.

With single stream (commingled) recycling, some cities now allow everything - metal, glass, mixed paper and plastic - in the same recycle bin for pick-up, but some cities still require source (home) separation.

I ran through the front door of the shelter. Cathy, the veterinarian, was feeding the rabbits.

"Hi, Cathy!" I called. "Have you seen Bubbles?"

"Hi, Tiana! Yes, I did. I fed her a treat when I took out our recyclable materials. Then she dashed off behind the recycle truck going toward the service station."

We helped Cathy make a sign about Bubbles on recycled paper and posted it in her window.

"Thanks!" I said. "I hope we find her soon."

"I'm sure you'll catch up to her soon!" Cathy said.

"Come on, kids," Mom said. "Let's go to the service station. Bubbles loves to play on the tire pile there. See you later, Cathy."

RECYCLE YOUR CAR PARTS!

We collect car metal, batteries and even oil from the car's engine.

We recycle them carefully so the chemicals won't harm people or the earth.

CAR METAL

Batteries

The service station attendant waved as we drove up.

"Hi, Mr. Lindsay," I called. "Have you seen Bubbles?"

"You just missed her, Tiana. I went to get her some water while she played on the tire pile, but when I came back, she'd gone. She was chasing the recycle truck toward the park."

"Oh, no!" I moaned. "We just missed her again, Mom!"

"I think we're getting closer," Mom said. "The park's the last stop before the MURF."

We thanked Mr. Lindsay for his help.

"I hope you find Bubbles. I'll keep an eye out for her."

At the park, we searched all the places Bubbles usually played. No luck.

Before long, I saw our neighbor.

"Hey, Mr. Gibbs!" I called. "Have you seen Bubbles?"

"Hi, folks! Yes, I just saw her playing with the other dogs under that tree."

"There she is!" Peter shouted. He pointed toward the street. "And she's going toward the MURF!"

We jumped back in the car and drove after her.

When we arrived at the MURF, we called and whistled, but we couldn't see Bubbles anywhere.

We quickly dropped off our recyclable materials in each collection bin and kept looking around.

Soon a worker walked out.
"Hi, Mr. Bailey," Peter called. "We're looking for Bubbles. She ran this way, chasing a recycle truck. Have you seen her?"
"Nope, but we can search inside."

"Wow!" I exclaimed. "This place is awesome!"

"How about a tour while we look for your dog?" Mr. Bailey offered.

"What a terrific idea!" Mom agreed.

"OK, great. Everyone put on hard hats and come with me."

"Out here, we feed all the recyclable materials—the plastic and paper and stuff—onto that long conveyor belt. It's like a train. It carries everything inside the building where it'll all be sorted."

The weight shows what to pay the MRF for processing the recyclable materials or how much the MRF owes your city. The fee depends on the market price of the recyclable material; prices always go up and down like other products on the stock market. Paper prices change a lot because it's what gets recycled most.

WEIGHING STATION

What a racket!

"What's that?" I asked, pointing to a big machine.

"That's called a Hopper. The recyclable materials sit inside there before moving on to sorting. Do you know how they are sorted?"

Tour Information:
Different Materials Recovery Facilities/Recycling Centers may sort materials in different ways. When you go to other cities, visit the MRF to see how they sort recyclable materials.

TIPPING FLOOR

TRASH SKIP

MAIN SORTER

PLASTICS BELTS

Mr. Bailey sure knows a lot about this stuff.

Newer MURF's may use optical sorters to sort glass.

⑤

"Plastics tumble through an optical sorter. That's a ray of light that tells their plastic type, such as clear PET #1 or color HDPE #2. Their conveyor belt rolls them to the plastic collection bins.

The sorter also separates other plastic types like PVC #3, PP #5, PS #6, and OTHER #7, which are growing markets."

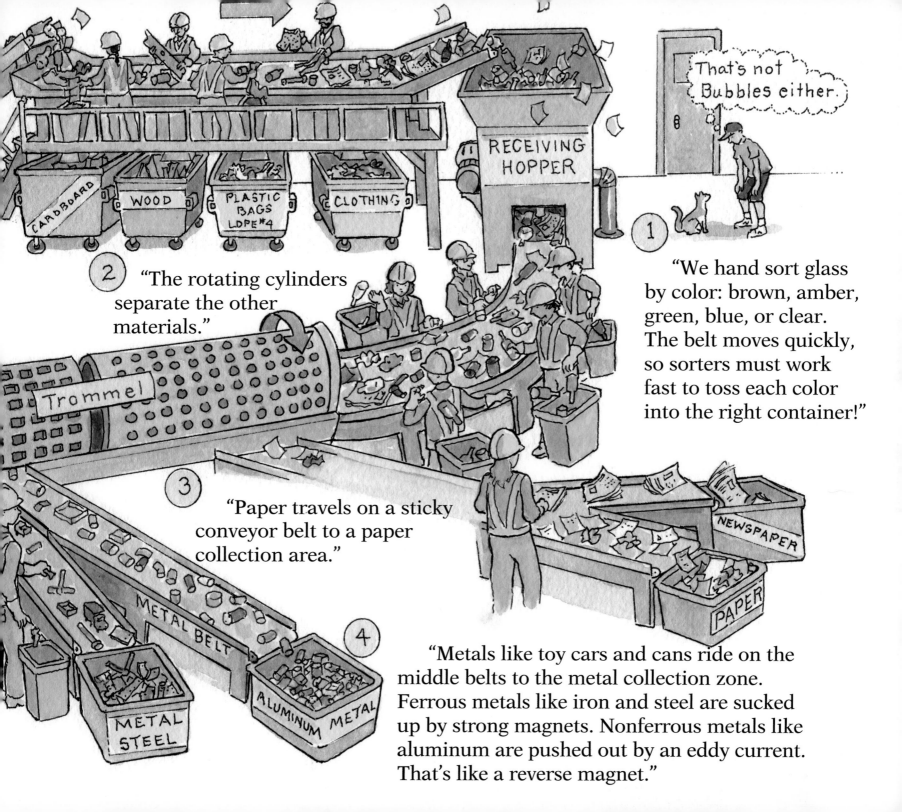

"After sorting, we squash each material into bales, which we sell and ship to factories that make them into new things like newspapers, beverage cans, bottles and even t-shirts. It's a lot of work, but recycling saves in many ways."

CHUG

RATTLE

CLINK

CRACKLE

SNAP

Paper bales are shipped to paper mills.
Aluminum bales are shipped to aluminum manufacturers.
Steel bales are shipped to scrap metal dealers and steel mills.
Glass pieces are shipped to a glass processing plant.
Plastic bales are shipped to plastic manufacturers.

Suddenly, I heard a rustling sound nearby. A moment later, I saw a shiny, black nose poking out between two bins.

"Bubbles!" I shouted. "Look, everyone! She was hiding in a collection bin! Come, Bubbles!"

Bubbles jumped out, trotted into my arms, and licked my cheeks.

"Bubbles! We were worried about you!" Mom said, as she fed her a treat from her pocket.

"Hey, girl!" Peter said, "You sure know where recyclable materials go, don't you? You know what we can call you? Bubbles, The Recycle Dog!"

We all laughed as we climbed into the car. Bubbles jumped into the back seat next to Peter.

"Next stop, the groomer," I said. "I bet Mr. Mendez would love to hear about our recycling adventure with Bubbles. And maybe he'll show us how he recycles too!"

Up to 70-80% of the waste that ends up in the
average waste bin could be recycled.

On average, around 16% of the money you
spend on a product pays for the packaging,
which ultimately ends up as waste.

Up to 95% of a vehicle can be recycled.
The 80% that's steel and 15% other materials.

Every ton of mixed paper that is recycled can save
the energy equivalent of 185 gallons of gas.

Recycling one aluminum can saves enough energy
to run your TV for three hours.

For Reflection

1. What happened in this story? Discuss with others.
2. What lessons did you learn?
3. Do you and your family recycle?
4. Has your dog ever chased a truck?
5. Has your dog ever been lost? What happened?
6. Have you ever visited a Materials Recovery Facility?
7. Apply the lessons you learned to real situations. Set new goals.
8. What could you do to increase recycling in your home and community?

Be a Garbologist

What is Garbology?

Garbology, a small niche of archeology, is the scientific study of waste and the way it reflects upon the lifestyles of a group of people. A garbologist is a person who studies waste by examining its effect on humans and society.

Follow the steps below to investigate waste impacts in your community.

1. Awareness of the Issues: Discover a *collection or sorting* issue in your community. Analyze it to determine what makes it an issue. Identify different sides of the issue and the factors that affect it, such as personal values, business, the economy, cultural values and beliefs.

2. Investigation: Identify a *collection or sorting* issue in your community and gather information about it using questionnaires, surveys, interviews and other techniques in order to understand all sides of the issue. Review the information and try to come up with two or three possible solutions.

3. Solutions: Brainstorm the solutions. Weigh them and select the course of action that seems most practical.

Experiments and Activities

Sorting: Recyclable Materials versus Trash

This exercise will help you learn to sort products in different ways.

What you need: Seven small cardboard boxes; a marker; some trash and other products, such as an empty pickle bottle (brown, green, clear or blue), an empty ketchup bottle, empty pop cans, paper, a chocolate wrapper, an empty egg carton, newspaper, a magazine, an empty milk carton, a gum wrapper, a flower pot, batteries, shoes, a hairspray can, etc.

What to do: Label the boxes with the marker: Plastic, Glass, Aluminum, Steel & Tin, Paper, Trash, Miscellaneous. After the boxes have been labeled, sort the products, placing each one in the appropriate box. Explain why you put them there.

Tip: You can do this at home with your own trash.

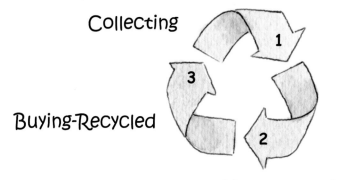

Collecting

Buying-Recycled

Manufacturing

1

3

2

Closing the Loop

Look at the recycle symbol on this page. What do the three chasing arrows mean? For recycling to succeed, new products made from recycled materials must be purchased and used! Look around your house and classroom and identify items made out of recycled materials.

What else can you do to close the loop? Perhaps you could start a local collection program in your community. Can you think of anything else? Make a list of all your ideas.

Note to Parents, Teachers and Librarians

Congratulations! Your child has taken the first step to learning about Environmental Science and Sustainability. The EcoAdventures™ imprint is designed to introduce young readers to key concepts while challenging them to think about the world around them. Simultaneously, it augments their reading library with educational stories and books.

Read Think Do™

The EcoAdventures™ set of books is a valuable addition to the home, classroom and library. Stories are designed to be read aloud to children, as well as to be read by a child independently. Images and definitions throughout the books are aids to learning the key concepts. The fun facts and practical lessons following each story stimulate children to think about the environment. Their understanding is strengthened by a hands-on project at the end. These books help children learn to question, analyze and interpret what they see; gain an understanding of environmental processes and systems; understand and address environmental issues; and learn about personal and civic responsibility.

EcoAdventures™ Garbology Kids™ Series

The EcoAdventures™ Garbology Kids™ Series uses humor to encourage greater learning and broader thinking about material waste, waste generation, waste management and waste technologies. It includes diagrams of the materials recycling loop and the waste management hierarchy. It also explains the most common principles of waste management, diversion and disposal: the chief Recycling Concepts (the 3 R's: Reduce, Reuse, Recycle), Transform, Treatment and Disposal.

Materials Recycling Loop

The recycle symbol shows three chasing arrows. Each arrow represents a step in the recycling loop—collecting, manufacturing and buying recycled products. When all three are done, we "close the recycling loop."

1. Collecting
When you place a plastic bottle (and other recyclables) in a bin, it is taken to a material recovery facility (MRF) - the MURF. There the products are sorted by type and compressed into bales.

2. Manufacturing (Processing)
Factories mix paper with water to make pulp, and melt the metals, glass and plastic in high heat to make molten liquid. Then they make raw materials, like pellets or flakes, or new products like bottles.

3. Buying-Recycled
The new products are distributed to stores to be bought and recycled again.

Waste Management Hierarchy

The waste management hierarchy classifies waste management strategies according to the order of importance and desirability. Follow the Garbology Kids™ Series to learn about each level of the waste management hierarchy.

Most Preferred Option

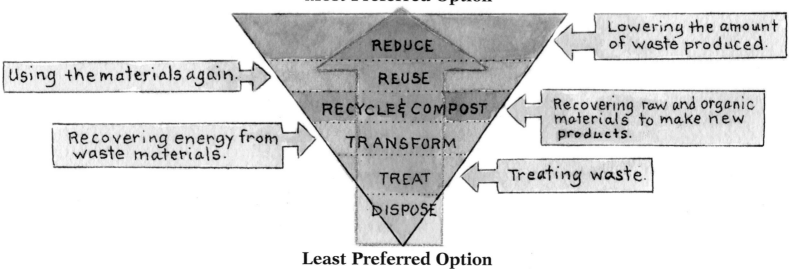

Least Preferred Option